VERDANT VERSES

NEETI PARTI

Made with ♥ on the Notion Press Platform
www.notionpress.com

Contents

RHYTM DIVINE

1. A Pilgrimage To The Inner Self — 3
2. I Love Dark Nights — 5
3. Dream Of The New Born — 7
4. Dawn Of Hope — 9
5. Ganga, Mother Of All — 11
6. Dynamic Dawn — 13
7. Dance Of The Aurora Borealis — 14
8. Soaring High In Love Eternal — 16
9. The Song Of The Butterfly — 18
10. Shaded Visions — 20
11. Bounties Of Nature Are Free — 22
12. A Ray Of Hope — 24
13. Rhythm Divine — 25
14. Salmon Eruditions — 27
15. Sing To Me Nightingale — 29
16. Snowflake — 31
17. Heavenly Wings — 33
18. In Tune With The Lotus Leaf And The Blue Butterfly — 35
19. Green Romance — 37
20. Hope — 39
21. I Am A Child, I Want To Fulfil Your Dreams — 40
22. I Am A Happy Rainbow — 42
23. Reawakening — 44

Contents

24. Light Up My World — 46

25. Mother Dolphin's Insight — 48

26. Song Of Nature — 50

27. In Defence Of Myself — 52

28. One Whom I Love — 54

29. Cry Of The Ozone Layer — 56

30. Peaceful Whispers — 58

31. The Flowers You Sent Me — 59

32. The Holy Ganges And I — 61

33. Blue Bonding — 63

34. We Are The Enlightened — 64

35. Withering Petals — 66

36. Heritage — 68

I AM DESTINY'S OFFSPRING

37. I Am A Figment Of Others' Imagination — 73

38. A Vision Of My Own Imagination — 76

39. A Handful Of Sky — 78

40. Contemplation — 79

41. Courage — 80

42. Course Of Life — 81

43. Creation Holds Me In Loving Embrace — 82

44. Fading Footprints — 83

45. I Am The Chosen One — 85

46. Behind Closed Doors — 87

Contents

47. It Cannot Be — 89

48. I Am A Woman Of Substance — 91

49. I Am Destiny's Offspring — 93

MUSINGS & MORE

50. Nostalgia — 99

51. A Long Walk To Freedom — 100

52. Anger In Control — 102

53. Hear My Call — 103

54. Compassion – A Trending Fashion! — 104

55. Ferrying Future — 106

56. Paper Boat Dreams — 107

57. There's Wonder In Everything I See — 109

58. Death — 110

59. Feeding The Devil — 111

60. True Euphoria — 113

61. Expectation — 115

62. Eyes Say It All — 117

63. Forging Women Power — 119

64. Garden Of Education — 121

65. Clouds Of Imagination — 123

66. The Highway Diaries — 124

67. Ignite A Spark — 126

68. Images And Invocation — 128

69. The Pursuit Of Love — 130

Contents

70. It's All About Pride 132

71. Jung-e-vairav, The Saga Of The Brave Parsi Women 134

72. Immortal Love 137

73. Language, Literature And Society: Quest For Utopia! 139

74. Lohri: The Joyful Blaze Of Harvest 142

75. Life Is A Mirage 145

76. Life Our Greatest Teacher 146

77. We Shall Overcome 147

78. Visions Of Lavender 149

79. Brooming Beats 151

80. Growing From Strength To Strength 153

81. Love At First Sight 155

82. Eternal Love 157

83. Luminescent Future 159

84. I Can Feel You 161

85. Glorious Autumn 163

86. Mahan Aatma 165

87. Monochrome City 167

88. My Sunshine 169

89. Choose To Be A Seraphim 171

90. Olive Green:the Colour Of Unity In Diversity 173

91. Open Your Arms To Joy 175

92. No One Knows My Pain – I Do! 177

93. Paradise 179

Contents

94. Paths And Destinations — 181

95. Peace — 183

96. Power Of Thoughts — 184

97. It's All About Pride — 186

98. The Next Chapter — 188

99. Triumph Over Saomai — 190

100. In Conversation With The Winter Breeze — 193

101. Someday, Somewhere — 195

To

My son – my sunshine

"Poetry is when an emotion has found its thought and
thought has found words."
– Robert Frost.

RHYTM DIVINE

1. A PILGRIMAGE TO THE INNER SELF

In the land of yonder
I once was drawn by the mystery
Unfolding in the clear flowing waters
Mystical waters, life giving waters

Floating in suspension on the shimmering aqua surface
Was a broad leaf with diamond drops glowing on it's jade skin
Carried along by the waves it was ethereal and peaceful
On the ultimate journey to meet the mighty ocean, unmindful
and free!

Fighting mightily with the rhythmic flow
Taking leaps above the rippling surface, against the current
Were scores of glistening, wide eyed, determined salmon
On their tragic yet exhilarating, fatal but life-giving voyage

The leaf and the salmon moved towards their ultimate desire
Their soulful odyssey defining their conduct: similar goal,
antithetical means
Am I a leaf that rises above the struggles?

Or the salmon who will rest at peace after a struggle?

Peace with self was the spiritual craving
I searched for my soul to speak
My answer was writ large in the undulating wavelets
My spirit would reign supreme, conquer the challenge of life's
ripples I must!

2. I LOVE DARK NIGHTS

I long for dark nights that embrace
Scintillating, glimmering legion of coruscating heavenly stars
Winking at me invitingly to a mesmerising trance
While the eventide breeze ferries my adoration skywards

Crickets form a divine orchestra and sing in pulsating rhythm
Fireflies set the night ablaze in a choreographed luminescent
dance
Lakes mirror the enthralling celestial illustration
The crescent moon glows in regal radiance

Constellations form kaleidoscopic patterns on the empyrean
canvas
Galaxies capture in their album for posterity this wonder cosmic
My heart glows as it encapsulates the ethereal brilliance
And become one with the shimmering arcadia beatific

A gossamer orison comes cascading down
The night sky shares its dream sublime
An invocation to be free of choking pollution

Of forever being velvety caliginous till the end of time!

3. DREAM OF THE NEW BORN

*Eyes dancing, an endearing smile on his rosy mouth curving up
to dimpled cheeks*
*The baby gurgled merrily, kicked his tiny legs and waved his soft
arms about*
*His Nurturer looked on fondly "What makes you so happy my
little wonder?"*
*"Let me sing to you while I rock you to sleep my darling" she
whispered softly*

*A marvel of nature, her little bundle of joy drifted away into a
world of dreams*
*His mind moving into an undefined dimension filled with
multihued visions;*
*Visions imprinted upon his unaware consciousness from time
immemorial*
*Like swirling clouds they whirled, twirled and pirouetted in
symphony*

*The sunrise stains of pink, orange and red like a painter's palette
gone wild*

Trees in emerald, jade, olive, teal swaying in the cool, refreshing breeze
Air filled with soothing sounds of tweeting, whistling and chirping of birds
The infinite azure blue sky with a brilliant rainbow running across it's expanse

Winding rivers bubbling, splashing, tumbling while carrying glassy waters
Deep, swelling seas with frilly, foam edged lofty waves falling upon the land
Seasons changing: ochre summer, flaming autumn, green spring and white winter
Happy children of all ages playing in fields without fences and spaces unbound

The doting mother sensed it all and a dark shadow of guilt fell upon her face
Tears filled her eyes, she looked heavenwards and a silent prayer escaped her lips
"Give us all the gift of selflessness and courage, O Lord, so we may create a world
Where peace may nurture growth of free spirit and inspire universal brotherhood!"

4. DAWN OF HOPE

Incensed breeze blows languidly through the trees
Awakening the five senses
And the soul within
Ah, what unparalleled bliss!

Leisurely, the sky tuns a gentle pink
As the apricot sunrays peek through
Like a newlywed bride blushing
While stealing a look at her soulmate

A black swallow tail butterfly
With flame-coloured speckles flutters past
Leading my eyes to the exotic sight of the purple sunbird
Glimmering in metallic blue with maroon feathers on the breast

I spot a cumulus sail teasingly by
As it winks at the sun
Brilliant gold rays set it on fire
Framing its gently curved edges in shimmer

The multi-hued bronze, orange and gold sky
Is illuminated with a message celestial

Believe in the Divine
And keep Hope alive!

5. GANGA, Mother of all

Avimukta, Anandvana, Mahashamshana, Kashi, Varanasi
Names of my first born
My favourite among all children
Whose side I have flown by and will till eternity

Swirling clouds make the night air thick with incensed fragrance
The fires in brass diyas dance, throwing arms of burning light
and glowing embers
Their frolic caught in the glowing kohl lined eyes of young
maidens
Cymbals clash in rhythm with the rising crescendo of chants
Enchanted pilgrims stare awestruck in disbelief
'Ganga, our mother we offer our humble tribute!'

The darkness in the east gracefully gives way to light......
Fires of another nature begin to kindle, taking on a ferocious
mode in no time
Reflections of saffron fall upon my waters through the day till the
west turns a deep pink
All consuming, yet all liberating Fires
Forming a heavenly path of souls on their final journey

Completing the ever-rotating ritualistic cycle of life…….

In the din I cry to those I nurture at my bosom
Wash your sins, not your filth
Cleanse your heart not your bodies
Try hard the powers that are
And spend all the monies
Continue to fail they will till
Till thine will wills it

Desecrate not my dignity, my purity, my life, my purpose
Allow me to remain clean, pure and divine
Hold me dear as I do you
Our lives are eternally conjoined
A mother does not wish ill her own
My own, me you must not disown, for I am mother of all!

6. DYNAMIC DAWN

When you see stark darkness
Outside your tiny window
Remember there are stars studded within
Find their light and draw inspiration

Keep your focus on the brightness
Allow not blackness to consume you
The Present is progressive and volatile
Time shifts the overwhelming dunes of sand

It is the destiny of the Horizon
To overcome the night of tribulations
And welcome the new Dawn
Born of new Hopes and Promises!

7. DANCE OF THE AURORA BOREALIS

The dark northern celestial sphere
Tenebrous, sinister, bleak, forbidding
Like an empty surface of a canvas waiting to find life
Through the vivid imagination of the Creator

The Universe urges the Celestial Sphere and the Earth
To choreograph a dance to cosmic strains
To overwhelm the blackness
As though it never existed

Heaven and Earth answer the call…

Swirling spirals of neon splash across the firmament
Carmine, scarlet, crimson, jade, emerald
Lime, aquamarine, yellow, violet, orange
The divine planetary palette
Overflows with hues unimaginable!

The empyrean vast becomes a shimmering kaleidoscope
Glowing spirits whirl and pirouette

In an intricate graceful aerial display
Of rhythmic, sensual, intoxicating manoeuvres
Elevating the soul to euphoric ecstasy

Incandescent Aurora, the Goddess of Dawn
Illuminate our creation,
Be our guiding light
Lead us on in righteousness
To eternal bliss in paradise!

8. SOARING HIGH IN LOVE ETERNAL

(A tribute to the inspiring true love of the Albatross)

Soaring high is my nature
I face the wind and fly upward
I shift and dip catching a draft
Rippling and blue as far as the eye can see
Below lies the mighty, heaving, rhythmic ocean
Homeward bound I am
In my search for my mate

Land ho! I glide into the feathered colony
It is time to dance, time to woo….
So many of us together prance and spring high
Slowly pairs move away into their own world
My eyes lock on a beauty. Our dance intensifies.
We move to the music of our own creation
I have found my soulmate!

Our gaze never wavering
We snuggle and preen.

We cavort, we frolic, we pirouette
Reaching a crescendo, we move and unite as One
And then gently embrace accepting each other for life
Together we shall live forever and ever, till Death do us apart!

9. THE SONG OF THE BUTTERFLY

I am a baby butterfly
Asleep in my cocoon
Unmoving I will lie
The sun shines or the moon

In the twinkling of an eye
I will take new birth
The cosmos I will beautify
To prove to all my worth

My aim is happiness
For every earthly soul
To remove all sadness
Be it child or the old

I live with the flowers
Selfless is my love
I sip honey nectars
And receive blessings from above

NEETI PARTI

My life is my message
I enchant with my wing
Let harmony in each heart reside
Songs of eternal peace I sing!

10. SHADED VISIONS

I dream in myriad hues holding shaded visions within a balloon
Come morn I release one
And watch it float carrying my wish
As I whisper a prayer for it to reach its destination

I sent up a red balloon today wishing for love pure
Love to conquer and love for all ills to cure
Yesterday a yellow balloon had dotted the skies
It bonded with the energy of the sunrays
And the world seemed to be a better place

Green, the colour of nature did precede
The earth I am sure felt healed
Blue was the balloon that befriended the firmament
Assuring me it will attenuate all ailment
While the pink promised to be a nurturant

The orange I have been holding close to my heart
It has promised me energy and warmth
Balloons in white will be the companion
With each airship of aspiration

Every dream will be in need of its illumination

The globe of colour purple is powerful and eager
It will be the final messenger
To be the driving force that will ensure
All my dreams spread across the azure
To make my chimera of Utopia come true!

11. BOUNTIES OF NATURE ARE FREE

In the meadow green
Sat I, by the sparkling, splashing stream
Dangling my feet in the bubbling waters
Delicate verdant fronds floating along my side
The tiny goldfish nibbled by the shoreline

The breeze teased the wispy clouds
And ran its fingers through my dark curls
As sunshine embraced my smile
A tangerine butterfly landed on the jasmine
Fluttering her dainty wings as she drank sweet nectar

The cuckoo cooed the arrival of spring
Sparrows hopped merrily in the grassy patch
Music pleasant I heard at a distance
A song lilting with a steady beat
Followed keenly its path as it drew close

Appeared a young shepherd boy leading his herd
Sang he as though he had not a care in the world

His words rang out clear and strong
'The best things in life are free, he crooned
Surrounded by bounties of nature I began humming the melody
in concurrence!

12. A RAY OF HOPE

The stubborn thick black cloud
Presumed its undeterred and undisputed power
Blocked the path of sunshine
Let out a thunderous roar
And sent a bolt of lightening
To spread terror and fear

The sun waited patiently

The Winds of Change watched the story unfold
Before making an entrance grand

A sweep of gust
A powerful thrust
The stormy cloud lost its guts

The Sunbeam was in wait
Sent out a ray as a band of gold-
A Ray of Hope
That God still holds the world in His fold!

13. RHYTHM DIVINE

Languorous dreams under the Jacaranda
Petals of purple cascade down in an amethyst curtain
Blossoms spread fragrance of ambrosian honey
Leaves of emerald play cadence divine
Tinkling laughter wafts through the air
A child is blowing reed bubbles
Columns of effervescence swarm in spirals
Halting momentarily to whisper sweet nothings
Nature orchestrates music exquisitely euphonic
Globules of silver, stream a luminescent heavenly path
Carrying springtime dreams ensconced within
Flame coloured butterflies their winged escorts
Shimmering rays spread enchantment
Prismatic rainbows float on the aqua spheroids
Ambling languidly in a leisurely dance
Of glossy incandescence
White velvety cumulous absorbs them in a soft embrace
To coalesce with drizzle drops to quench earths thirst
Ruminations of perfection in beauty follow
Azure skies smile in salutation
Rhythm empyrean unfolds incessantly
Angels breathe blessings of peace

God is in His heaven
My cup of bliss overflows!

14. SALMON ERUDITIONS

Silver to behold

Studded with spots and crosses bold

The Latin word 'Salmo' gives me my name

It means 'to leap' and that is my claim

I understand that old must give way to new

I battle strong currents and rapids I pursue

As I spring upstream to spawn

My body changing bright red from the silver with which I was

born

My journey is arduous and strenuous

Of many brethren I bear the loss

But I am resilient and determined

To never give up trying, I teach mankind

Know that we all stand on the shoulders

Of those that won the combat before us

We shall also sacrifice our all

Leaving a rich legacy behind us

Pollution, overfishing, climate change cause distress
Our habitat is lost as we ride the crest
We are a keystone endangered species
Save us, have upon us mercies!

15. SING TO ME NIGHTINGALE

My own follies have caught up with me
My pride hath brought the fall
I disregarded and abused you
Now you seek recovery
By confining me in my abode
Surrounded by walls of shame
Listening to the sounds of self-rebuke

Come to the Window of my Soul Nightingale
Sing sweet songs of Revival

The earth will shine with sunrays of sprinkled gold
Nature's magical brush will liberally splash verdant hues
Bunches of flowers will sway in the gentle breeze
Sparkling brooks will dance down merry slopes
Woods will resonate with sounds of the wild
The rainbow will smile in curves of VIBGYOR
Birds in flight will carry the message of resurrection

Come to my Tree of Hope Nightingale

VERDANT VERSES

Sing melodies of Rebirth

To reach the core of Mother Earth
So that it may sprout in glorious splendour yet again!

16. SNOWFLAKE

Cascading softly from the Heavens above
Like silent blessings nestled in a prayer
Each a wondrous crystal formed perfectly by divinity
The trees hold wide their branches for resting space
The earth opens its arms to welcome each flurry flake

A symbol of purity, a harbinger of beatitude
A metaphor for selfless giving, an allegory illustrating
magnanimity
Drawn towards children peeping from windows
Snuggle up on window sills
To form tiny milky mounds

A new dawn waits to arrive
Turning pink with excitement
To unveil the season of merriment that will bring unveiled joy
As footprints of younglings
Shall adorn the white carpet to shape fluffy balls

Snowmen with carrot noses and stick arms
Adorned with old hats and mufflers
Will smile in crooked smiles

Laughter unrestrained shall reach up to the blue skies
Empyrean will assign benedictions divine!

17. HEAVENLY WINGS

The Aravallis were so young and proud once
Having risen in multiple folds spanning our north-western front
They were witness to royal kings, bloody battles and conspiracies
Till time wore them out and they lay low and forgotten like an
old grandparent

Visible from my balcony view point
They evoked pity as one saw how they had been ravaged
Came the deadly virus bringing along with it a strange miracle
Birds aplenty came flocking to it as though returning into the
warm soft folds of their granny

I noticed the hillside changing hues
It was the plumage of Peacocks in a kaleidoscopic dance
Silent beauty ruled the moment as I stood mesmerised
Till the peculiar musical call of the Bulbul broke my reverie

As days passed more spectacular winged friends began filling my
world
Chirping of Sparrows, screech of Parakeets filled the morning air
instead of honks and horns

Greenish brown back with a perky upturned tail the ashy
Wren-Warbler
Could be found alongside the robin whistling a merry tune

The tiny Tailorbird would be flitting beside the teensy purple
Sunbird
The shy crow pheasant found a friend in the black Drongo
While the jungle Babbler would stir up a storm on spotting a
Black Kite
Warning of the impending danger to pairs of high-speed flying
Swallows

The evening would bring the two-toned Green Bee Eater and the
orange Hoopoe
The show stopper of the day would be the Kingfisher flashing his
brilliant blues
It was as if the heavens had opened up to remind us what man
had done to man
Came the realisation that our Pride in being infallible had
turned us willingly deaf and blind to Nature's healing beauty!

18. IN TUNE WITH THE LOTUS LEAF AND THE BLUE BUTTERFLY

***(This poem is inspired by the hydrophobic quality of the
lotus leaf and the wings of the blue butterfly)***

The breeze was the messenger of the clouds
It swept gently across my green garden small
And whispered in each ear of the arriving raindrops
Making their journey from beyond to bless us all

The sky began to spin out whirling clouds
Bringing gently rolling thunder in its wake
Released they their gathered silver rain drops
On thirsty flowers and leaves of green jade

Fell they in a shower with equal fervour
On the glassy pond veiled with lotus leaf
Along with a pretty butterfly azure of colour

Unbeknown to all both shared a common belief

The shining droplets descended on the cobalt butterfly
And they danced merrily on the paddle shaped lotus leaf
But could not the soak either surface even though they did try
Their endeavour to influence was futile and their stay was brief

Fragile looks the lotus leaf and the butterfly seems vulnerable
Hidden from all is their great strength and their resolve
Try with your power and bend their might you will not be able
With fortitude they face all adversity as firm they are of purpose
I looked on mesmerised and listened intently to my inner voice
To recognise my core values was Nature's intense message
Not chase others' false approval, be immune to those who criticise
Let fickle winds of opinion dissipate and let dignity define my
life!

19. GREEN ROMANCE

<u>*(On hugging a tree)*</u>

I watch spellbound
A bright blue and orange Kingfisher
Alight on your emerald green branches
While the mynah carries a twig
To build a nest for her offspring
A squirrel runs playfully up and down your arms.

I sit down in your fragrant shade
Upon the carpet of shed multi-hued leaves
While soft sunbeams dance upon your blossoms
The red-vented bulbul serenades me with her song
The cool breeze plays with my hair
Bliss is made of this!

I lose track of the passing time....
As I rise to leave
Your branches hold on to my scarf
You and I form an unspoken bond
Mutual affection surfaces
I embrace you

And promise to be your friend forever!

20. HOPE

A dark cloud with a silver lining
A light at the end of the tunnel
The pitter patter of raindrops
To assuage the thirst of a parched earth
Gold rays of sunshine
After a dark moonless night
Silvery moonlight on a full moon day
The fragrance of a flower
The caress of a cool breeze
The song of a bird hidden in leafy greens
The dance of a peacock
The sprouting of a new seed
The tinkling laughter of a child
The warm hug of a mother in troubled times
The bubbling sounds of a brook tumbling down a hill
The sight of a butterfly in flowery bowers
Fireflies glowing in pitch blackness
Are all heavenly messages of Hope writ large
Like a multi-hued rainbow shimmering across the skies
Ensuing a thundery downpour!

21. I AM A CHILD, I WANT TO FULFIL YOUR DREAMS

*I want to breathe fresh air and smell the flowers, I wear a
pollution mask*
*I want to play unhindered; I am put in enclosures with
unlimited caution*
*I wish to float in the waters of free-flowing rivers, I swim in a
pool with chemicals*
*I want to eat fresh healthy fruit; I get tasteless produce covered
with pesticide*
*I want to drink clean water; I consume plastic along with
bottled liquid*

*You heard tales of Ramayana and Mahabharata from your
Grannies*
*I want to hear them too, you say you are occupied and ask me to
watch cartoons*
*I find this world fascinating and want to ask questions; you say
you are busy*
*I wish to be home to share my thoughts, you ask me to make
friends at 'Day Care'*

I desire to cuddle up, look into your eyes and feel warm, you say
you are tired

The world looks at me and believes that I will work wonders
The sun will shine brighter, not hidden behind a haze
The sky will be blue and devoid of smoke from burning farms
There will be good health, prosperity and happiness
Brotherhood will prevail and love will be the universal language

I will give back manifold your investment in me
Fill me with your love, understanding and trust
Allow me to soak in knowledge from far and wide
Let me fall, rise, fall yet again and rise stronger
I am your child; I want to fulfil your dreams!

22. I AM A HAPPY RAINBOW

I am a Happy Rainbow
I am shaped like a smile

I appear on the horizon
When the sky feels joy

Seven are my colours
Together called **VIBGYOR**

Violet is made of red and blue
It is the colour of royalty true

Indigo is the colour that brings hope new
Vastness is the meaning of this deep blue

Blue is fifth in line
The colour of all that is divine

Green at the centre brings us wealth

With it's friends happiness and good health

Yellow is bright, golden and awesome
It speaks of lots of energy and wisdom

Orange is like a burning flame
Sparkling, playful and warm like its name

Red is on the top and a colour that is smart
It teaches us to love everyone with all our loving heart!

23. REAWAKENING

I looked at the flower of my life one fateful day
It turned towards me and it's eyes filled with hot tears
'My petals have lost colour, they have withered, are shrivelled
and drooping
I need rain and sunshine or I am going to die!' it said.

I searched the core of my heart and found deep corrosive anger
living within
My self-conceit had expected and demanded that everything
work as per my design
Negativity simmered because others had not measured up to my
expectation
I had let resentment define me, crippling my wellbeing
Spitefulness, revenge and bitterness had overshadowed my
spirituality
It was time for my ego to relinquish and align my life to the
Higher Truth......
And almost instantaneously, as though by miracle, it began to
rain!

As my moral chaos began untangling, I looked inwards at my
own actions

I found deep destructive fear living within
I was in agony over my inability to live up to the expectations of
others
I had let the pain of humiliation define me, crippling my
healing
Remorse, guilt and overpowering shame had blinded my inner
self
I surrendered my all to the Omniscient and the Omni-
benevolent.....
And at that instant, as though by action Divine, the sun began
to shine!

The ailing flower of existence turned heavenwards to receive the
blessed rain and sunshine
Peace descended upon my soul, revealing the path of inner
devotion: the path of life itself!

24. LIGHT UP MY WORLD

*Breaking away from the shimmering stars of the midnight blue
sky
You made a descent to adorn the wide terrestrial carpet in
summers
Carrying within you a Godly light that lit up our very souls
Caught in the brilliance of your glow, the earth would gleam
and glimmer*

*Lighting the rich green foliage running along the waters of calm
ponds
Your shining display could be seen forming magical patterns on
trees
You twinkled over the farmers' fields, your silent tribute to his
toil
Grassy patches would come alive with your scintillating presence*

*How I lament over the inhuman actions of the most superior of
beings
Harsh glares of haphazardly placed blinding lights occupy your
domains*

*Piles of callously thrown rubbish fills the shallow waters you
brought to life
We have taken away your canopied haunts and created a
'concrete' earth*

*Oh beautiful Firefly, my heart yearns for your radiant
luminescence
I search in vain for you to light up the dark, hazy and empty
skies
Like a child my eyes long for your winged fairy like presence
For you taught us that if you are true at heart, you light up the
world!*

25. MOTHER DOLPHIN'S INSIGHT

Mother Dolphin had taken Baby Dolphin
For a watery trek
When they found themselves
Facing a shipwreck
Broken into many pieces
It lay surrounded by riches
Baby Dolphin started to cry
As sad was the sight
Mother Dolphin understood the child's plight
And decided to give her an insight
To know wrong from right
This sunk ship teaches us a lesson
Do give me a listen
Many a threat you will face
Allow fear not near
Abandon not hope
Stay strong and be bold
Whenever Destiny throws challenges in your life
Remember this sunken ship and fight with all your might
My blessings will protect you all the while

You will emerge the winner!

26. SONG OF NATURE

The gentle zephyr affectionately caressed the cuckoo
Overcome by emotion, the ebony black bird responded with a
melodious 'kooo-ooo'
'Witt-witt splee-plink' sang the fork tailed barn swallows, as
their blue backs shone in sunshine
Infected by melody, 'chiddik- chiddik' went the house sparrows
continuing to build their nest
'Hoooah hoo hoo hoo chirry chirry chirry choreeo' joined in the
dove
The mynahs screeched loudly as they took off in pairs to search for
scraps
'Pia ow ey awe' yowled the peacock loudly
To which the rose ringed parakeet whistled a sweet warning
The excited cat mewed in response to the multitude of sounds
Annoying the flock of Jungle Babblers who launched into a
litany of admonishing harsh chirps
The chameleon nodded in agreement as it turned green within
the leafy surrounds
The squirrel scrambled up and down the Gulmohar chattering
incessantly in happiness
The metallic blue, purple and maroon sunbird hummed a tune
as it fluttered from flower-to-flower sipping nectar

'Charr charr' chipped in the Woodpecker as it drummed a tattoo
into the teak
Multihued butterflies flapped colourfully as they lighted on
inviting blossoms
The red wattled lapwing walked around in a lady like manner
surveying all that was happening

A toddler heard the live orchestra and gurgled in delight
Prompting her parents to look up from their laptops and laugh
at the sight
The gentle zephyr came by again and carried exultation far and
wide
Bearing the music of nature on its wings light!

27. IN DEFENCE OF MYSELF

I am a mushroom also known as a Toadstool
It seems I offer the toad a perfect seating stool

I am a fungi
Indeed, I am a fun guy
I simply sprout out from the ground
So, I am grounded too

Jokes apart…
Did you know of literature I am a part
And a concept for beautiful art?

Not only
Am I an integral part of Alice in Wonderland
I form the theme for Sir Joshua Reynolds
I was portrayed as a seat for Puck
For Shakespeare's play illustrations!

Henry Fuselli followed it up with 'Tatiana's Awakening'

Mine is the surface upon which fairies, sprits, and creatures
assemble
Mesmerising is the brushwork of light and shadows
Depicting love in two aspects
Light portrays carefree love; Darkness represents the erotic!
You have to agree I am exotic

And mystical too

I can tell you more tales of wonder…

Look for me in magical greens
For I grow in Fairy rings!

28. ONE WHOM I LOVE

My attraction, my love is unconditional and eternal
I am drawn to you like a magnet
From the moment I open my eyes
Your presence lights up my life

O Rising Sun, you are the one whom I love!
I watch your rosy radiance spread over the horizon
Like the blush of a newly wedded bride
Like a painter's canvas turning carmine with each crimson
stroke

Icy mountain tops transform into a treasure-box of glittering
rubies
While rippling waters choreograph your brilliant effulgence
Into golden vermillion tinted life-giving elixir
That goes tumbling down to the wine-red seas

Gentle rays of pink sunbeams reach out to night dew
Warming it into invisible vapours
That hover over rooftops like softly whispered prayers

On their journey to heavenly paradise

Untiring, pertinacious, devoted, unwavering
Persistent, indefatigable, dedicated, selfless
You are life sustaining, benevolent and vernal
An inspiration for all mankind!

29. CRY OF THE OZONE LAYER

Dear earthlings, safe, ensconced you were
Within your progenitor Mother Earth
And the vast blue umbrella of the Sky
Unbeknownst to all I was the protective lining
The invisible and silent Ozone layer, proud of my role as a
protector

You grew arrogant and greedy
Your uncouth, uncaring attitude began piercing my soul
Your relentless hammering cut through my very being
Your intrusions have left bleeding gashes on me
Allowing harmful UV rays through, damaging all life forms and
causing cancer

Are you so blind as not to see that remedy is urgent?
Repent and repair your erroneous lifestyle
Avoid consuming CFCs, halogenated hydrocarbon, methyl
bromide and nitrous oxide
Bike, carpool, walk and decrease the use of cars, maintain air
conditioners

Go Green

Is that too much to ask the custodians of generations to come?

• 57 •

30. PEACEFUL WHISPERS

Goddess Iris spread her rainbow arc on the gold horizon
The dark thunder clouds receded after shedding a shower
The earth sighed happily as it drank in large gulps
Winding thread like streams rolled happily downhill
The raindrops resting on the green leafy oak tree
Sparkled like diamonds as they reflected nature's bonanza
The wet bird sheltering in the leafy branches ruffled her wings
Sending a fresh fine spray of drops on the tulip cluster
Happiness of interdependence reigned supreme
As the cool breeze whispered the message of Peace!

31. THE FLOWERS YOU SENT ME

Petals so bright
Seeking brilliant sunshine
Like gold in shining light
The sunflowers resting in velvety greens so fine

Your bouquet to me as we were betrothed
Flower that I had always loved
In a crystal vase they stayed
Bringing a smile to each who upon it gazed

Preserved the seeds for later
Scattered them in the ground in winter
Nurtured by the sun and water
Tiny saplings appeared from the earth, our mother

Nature's magical gift
My heart and spirits they did lift
Grew they tall and upright
Wondrous flowers sprouted glittering even in moonlight

Squirrels danced around them in happy rhythm
Butterflies alighted upon them with a merry hum
Sunflowers beloved adorned my garden season after season
As my soulmate and I found greater love in our union!

32. THE HOLY GANGES AND I

<u>(Cry of the Ganga Dolphin)</u>

Ma Ganga is an embodiment of gentleness
She is a mother who absorbs the sins of her children
Her divinity is everlasting
She has provided me safe sanctuary since time immemorial
She was as pure as pure can be
Her crystal waters were my haven
Muddied they became
And I declared myself blind for survival
I am the Ganga Dolphin
I taught myself to hunt by emitting ultrasonic sounds

Atrocities on Ma Bhagirathi continued unabated
No difference did my sacrifice make

Entanglement in fishing nets as a bycatch
Hunted for oil, as bait for catfish
As liniment, as aphrodisiac and for meat
I continue to be exploited mercilessly

Endangered now
Both My Goddess and I
Beg for compassion
Pray for mercies
Allow us to survive and serve!

33. BLUE BONDING

Goddess Iris spread her rainbow arc on the gold horizon
The dark thunder clouds receded after shedding a shower
The earth sighed happily as it drank in large gulps
The raindrops resting on the green leafy oak tree
Sparkled like diamonds as they reflected nature's bonanza
The wet bird sheltering in the leafy branches ruffled her wings
Sending a fresh fine spray of drops on the tulip cluster
Happiness of interdependence reigned supreme
As the cool breeze whispered the message of Blue Bonding!

34. WE ARE THE ENLIGHTENED

Many a wise men speaks
Many a wisdom seeker listens
All caught in a cycle of finding ways
Which are straightforward
But somehow end up in a maze
Losing their path and subsequently themselves

We are The Enlightened!

Our city drains are choked
Floods have left behind a trail of dead
Children are drowning in open potholes
We shed tears for loss of human life
We lament the destruction of our Mother Earth
And keep destroying green to make luxury dwelling!

We are The Enlightened!
To reduce our sorrow
We plant saplings but leave taps running
To bring peace to our minds

We lecture our young but refuse to reuse
To assuage our guilt
We donate but do not recycle

We are The Enlightened!

What we put out there will come back to us
A universal truth unquestioned!
We Are Indeed The Enlightened!

35. WITHERING PETALS

Deep-red in colour, soft petals exquisitely curled at the ends
The gentle zephyr spread my heady fragrance
Attracting winged butterflies that romanced me, kissed me
passionately, confessing undying love
I flirted ceaselessly earning myself the title of Floret Casanova!

Not a cloud in the sky, with the sun in my eye
I was whispering sweet nothings to the tree nymph butterfly
He sat himself down on the blue corrugated-iron bench
frightening my delicate lover into flight

A deep sigh emanated and I detected the moisture in his eyes as
he spotted me
With a soft groan, he reached out and plucked me
"She loves me, she loves me not," he chanted plucking my petals
"She loves me not," he wailed as he came upon my last petal
leaving me withering on the ground

Prayers answered, velvety hands picked me up at sunset

I found myself in the folds of the frilly frock of a blue-eyed,
golden-haired angel
Pressed me in a book, preserved my shape and sweet scent
She carefully transferred me between transparent pieces of contact
paper
I was born again as a bookmark!

Granted eternal life I live in a fairy tale book
At starlight, she opens the page marked by me
Lovingly placing me beside her, she reads me a story
Till both of us drift off into the land of dreams!

36. HERITAGE

Sparkling sunshine, twinkling twilight
Green canopies beyond the blue
Song of the cuckoo brightened the summer
Fireflies lit up the night

Homes warm, streets abuzz
Sounds of merriment, children at play
Women in sarees bright, men riding bikes
Friendly gossip across walls, tasty dishes shared across

My heritage unquestioned
Defined my life pattern
Noiseless, menacing, moving stealthily
Came the dark clouds of destruction

Blurred mornings, smoggy evenings
Lost starlight, heaving earth
Blaring horns, speeding cars
Childhood confined to multitude of screens

I question my intent
I probe my actions

Was dismantling my Karma?
Did I wreck what I was entrusted with?

My answer comes from within
Mine was not to take but to value and add
It's time to repent, rebuild, restore, repair, revive
Our heritage to honourably bequeath!

I AM DESTINY'S OFFSPRING

Evidently the most difficult of questions to address is 'Who am I?'

It seems as though the canvas of our life is painted by others, while we stand at a distance trying to decipher the emerging, ever-changing picture of our own selves, and become 'a figment of others' imagination'.

This poem is my journey of self-realisation — of being a beautiful woman!

37. I AM A FIGMENT OF OTHERS' IMAGINATION

Obedient, honest, truthful, hardworking
Committed, submissive, respectful
Soft spoken and malleable
I am the perfect daughter
I must be so
Am I living up to the vision of your imagination?
I belong not here
I have to go elsewhere
Where?
Was this not home?

Subjugated, faithful, submissive
Self-sacrificing, ever smiling, uncomplaining
Sensitive to needs of all
I am the perfect wife
I must be so
Am I living up to the vision of your imagination?
I have come from elsewhere
Do I belong?

Here?
Is this my home?

Omnipresent, understanding, stoic, pliable
I am the daughter-in-law
I am the sister-in-law
I am the mother
I must be so
Am I living up to the vision of your imagination?
Who am I?
Where do I belong?

Yet from all directions I hear…
Discover yourself
Be true to yourself
Answer your calling
Know your potential
Define your happiness
I am a person
Who am I?
Where do I belong?

I try to search
I attempt to look deep inside
My endeavours meet with emptiness
And deafening silence
I have lost my way to myself

I see a blurred vision of self
I remain, a figment of others' imagination!

Deep inside us lies a unique wonder, a person that took all the
powers of the Universe to come into being, waiting to
emerge.........
This is how I found myself......

38. A VISION OF MY OWN IMAGINATION

Glanced at the mirror per chance
Saw a reflection that caught my interest
Who is that?
Stopped to get a better look
Hmmmm....
Not bad!
Sparkling dark eyes looked back
A smile followed

The desire to meet yet again began to grow
The heart grew fonder
The yearning became stronger
The mirror and the image began to merge
Acquaintance first
Then friendship
Now mutual admiration
A romance had begun......

It was time to look deeper

To go beyond and search the soul

A shimmer of light shone through
Darkness dissipated as though it had never existed
Deep inside lay a person
A woman undiscovered
Slowly she emerged
Shy and timid at first, then strong and resolute

Loving but independent
Kind but courageous
Confident but open minded
Humble but intellectually challenging
Ambitious but empathetic
Elegant, level headed
Trustworthy, hard working
Comfortable in her own skin

Disbelief and denial followed
The path to Acceptance was not easy
Slowly the guilt of self-discovery began to evaporate
Serenity and peace followed
Then elation
And Celebration
I am a beautiful woman!
I am a vision of my own imagination!!

39. A HANDFUL OF SKY

A dream to follow
A beating heart
An urge to prove

Self-belief
Trust in self
Respect aplenty

Firm
Undeterred
Resolute

The Universe will read your message
It will offer a handful of sky
Leading to an illuminated path
To fulfilment!

40. CONTEMPLATION

I peep out from my emotional window
To view my lot
With openness
And gratitude in my heart

Blessed am I
To be surrounded by loved ones
To have received knowledge limitless and unrestrained
To have been given the opportunity to impart my learnings

Life's experiences tell me
To shift focus from the wrinkles of time
Of obstacles faced and wishes unfulfilled
For I have much for which I am beholden!

41. COURAGE

Difficult to define
Is it within me and mine?

Is it
A rush of adrenaline,
A sustained emotion,
A momentous reaction?

A virtue imbibed,
A quality acquired,
An ethic inspired?

Definitely
A requirement
For life's fulfilment

May God grant it
May truth and honesty accompany it
Only then will life be worth it!

42. COURSE OF LIFE

As I sail the calm waters

Bathing in the radiant glow of the coral sunset

My soul searches for answers

Is this the true course of life?

Or do I row into turbulence

To be a part of the struggles

I may lose some battles

Perchance I may come out a winner

And help steer towards a win some others

43. CREATION HOLDS ME IN LOVING EMBRACE

The Universe smiled
And I was born!

I grow in the glow of the loving energy
Cosmos has bestowed upon me

My divine progenitor
I draw courage from your strong shoulders

I place my trust and my fate in your care
For struggles of life that lie ahead you prepare

Creation holds me in loving embrace
And looks over my shoulders

My life I owe to you I bow
I will make this world a better place I vow!

44. FADING FOOTPRINTS

Upright, graceful palm trees swayed in the breeze
Their outstretched branches welcoming the cool air
Stars in the velvet blue firmament
Created vivid patterns of constellations
The metronomic waves lapped gently against the shore
A rippling mirror to the starry skies.

I sat cross legged on the shore
Images of life playing upon my vision
My features displaying a range of expressions
As shadows of times flit past the mind's eye

I watched my fading footprints on the sand
As the lapping waves carried away their impressions
Layer by layer they dissolved into the vast embracing waters
An indication of time and tide waiting for none

I became aware of a smile upon my lips
It was time to let go of all that troubled
To allow cleansing ripples open doors to peace

Life would continue to test my strength
Shedding sorrows and allowing joys to thrive
Would make existence sublime!

45. I AM THE CHOSEN ONE

When the Universe smiles
A child is born
Nature's greatest tribute to itself
And Creations' trust in you

I became the chosen one

When I held you in my arms
A myriad of emotions flooded my being
A strange invisible bond formed

As I gathered you in my arms
You snuggled up against me
As acceptance of a tie eternal
Along with bliss of motherhood

Every minute thereafter has been blessed
Time and circumstances have tested us
You are my guide; I have tried to stay true

My efforts may have been worthy, yet I may have fallen short

My love for you is unconditional
With God by my side, I will continue to try
For my fallings I can only seek forgiveness
For the future I learn my lessons

You are a young man on the threshold of new beginnings now
May my prayers bring you peace and contentment
May happiness be your constant companion
May your cup of joy be always full!

46. BEHIND CLOSED DOORS

Behind closed doors
At the end of the day
I find no escape
From my own self

The exhausting day
Has been spent
Wearing various masks
It is difficult to peal the layers

With unmasking of each layer
I try to find myself
And keep losing my way yet again
Only to begin anew

The inner self knocks and mocks
It pushes me on
Asking a plethora of questions
About identifying my aspirations and dreams

The person in me refuses to accept anonymity
It seeks definition and action
I give in and listen to my own reflections
The journey to self-discovery has begun....

47. IT CANNOT BE

A large, heavy stone tied to my heart
Lead in my legs weighing me down
Tears waiting and watching
For time and space alone to flow
How could it be?!

Strong and steady
Faced many a storm
Never feared fate
Never shirked a call
Yet a sinking feeling now

The demeanour betrays no turmoil
All is well on the surface
The dark waters flow deep
The ripples are camouflaged with edges silver
A betrayal of self

Try as one might
To wear a mask
The mirror speaks the truth
And confronts me with it

In each reflection

It cannot be
I will not allow an exchange
Of duty and discipline
With nurturing feelings alien
That seem to have found a home in me

My acknowledgement is the beginning of the end
Rise I will
Win I will
Defeat shall follow
Deep determination

I seek Divine intervention
With the wind in my face
Resolve as my companion
I look for sunshine
So that the shadows may fall behind!

48. I AM A WOMAN OF SUBSTANCE

You hide me behind the purdah
You stifle my soul
You snatch away my freedom
You take away my identity
You muffle my voice

How insecure are you?
How great is your fear of my existence?
How scared are you of treating me as an equal?
How afraid are you of my independence?
How fearful are you of my strength?

Look into my eyes and face the truth

I am resilient
I am capable
I am pragmatic
I am reliable
I stand firm on my principles

I am a proud Woman of Substance!

49. I AM DESTINY'S OFFSPRING

I am destiny's offspring
The child of universal energy
Drawn towards the eastern sky as the pink dawn
I hang on to the luminescent horizon like the shining Morning
Star

My world lights up with the rising sun
Hope fills my being as the glorious day makes an appearance
A bird in flight carrying a twig flashes past the eye
A reminder of my harbourage built on labour of love

A selfish wispy cloud steals the sunshine
I know my day will be overcast by moving shadows
Blessed by Phoebus, I will ascend above the tribulations
And descend in the starlit alpenglow

To rise rejuvenated morn after morn!

MUSINGS & MORE

RECICPE FOR HAPPINESS POTION

INGREDIENTS:

- A Large Compassionate Heart
- Ample Forgiveness
- Abundant Gratitude
- Generous amounts of Generosity
- Plenty of Peace
- Sparkling Love full to the brim
- Good cheer for garnishing

METHOD OF PREPARATION:

Take the large compassionate heart and fill it with a healthy dose of all ingredients early in the morning.

Meditate for an hour to allow the flavours to intermingle.

Then garnish with good cheer.

PROCESS OF SERVING:

Ladle out copious portions to friends and family.

Donate charitably to those who seek.

Share portions aplenty with the needy to replenish the soul.

Sing songs of praise to the Almighty to reinvigorate.

Dance to the gifts of the world to spread joy.

Say a prayer of thankfulness before sleep to rejuvenate.

SECRET TIP:

Begin the process afresh each morning.

BENEFIT:

Enjoy good health and contentment all life through!

50. NOSTALGIA

Reflections melt in us leaving, a nostalgic sadness
And flow down as tears
Bringing a flood of despondent memories
Lingering on in the wrinkles of time

Hold close thou those ruminations
Those are treasures of moments past
Take a cautious peek now and then
To draw strength from them

Along with wisdom that comes
Riding on the back of Learning
Of falls and failures
Of descent and ascent

Know you that the cadence of Life
Would play no sentimental melodies
If reminiscent memories did not pull
At the strings of the heart!

51. A LONG WALK TO FREEDOM

With sunrise, the bustle would begin
The sound of the school bus crunchily halting on the gravel
The rush of uniformed children laughing and pushing to grab a
seat
Last minute stragglers running up with their parent shouting for
the driver to tarry

The girl would peek longingly out of the window as she waved to
her brother
Then she would turn away from the sunshine to her world of
darkness
The world of accumulated household chores
Her heart ached to be one amongst the morning crowd
But it was not to be. Girls did not need schooling
They were to marry and make their adopted family happy

No one understood her except for the old retired teacher next
door
She found every opportunity to be with her
In lieu, she would do clean and cook for her

Happy were the times of discovery and instruction

Sheer determination earned her acceptance to the world of
formal learning
It had been a long walk to freedom and enlightenment

Herself a teacher now, she knelt at the feet of the one who lit up
her world
With trembling hands, her mentor patted her head and blessed
her success in her mission:
The mission to self-respect and independence through education!

52. ANGER IN CONTROL

Anger, wrath, rage, fury
Uncontrolled emotions
That consume and destroy recklessly
Like a volcano that spews hot lava
Throwing up ash, fire and poisonous gas
Burning down everything in its way

It is like a candle burning at both ends
It wrecks the receiver
And ruins the perpetrator
Irrevocably destroys relationships
Leaving behind smouldering remains
Bitterness and Suffering

Be not ruled by it
Hold it on a leash
Release it on injustice and prejudice
Let it annihilate racism and bondage
Channelise it to defeat evil
And make this world a better place!

53. HEAR MY CALL

She knew how to go through the motions by now
Smile in place, fluid gestures, seemingly confident
Living up to everyone's expectations
Hiding her true self, waiting for the day to end

Later she would crumble
Fold up into a foetal position
Her body and mind shutting down completely
Putting her to long hours of slumber

Sleep was an escape away from reality
A way not to have to deal with herself
A state of being invisible
She did not want to wake up from

One among thousands, unable to articulate her manic depression
For fear of being condemned and shamed
Waiting to hear a soft reply of understanding
To help her call of help to find her life back again!

54. COMPASSION – A TRENDING FASHION!

The world is in need of Compassion
Let us make it a passion
Let us make it a trending fashion

May Compassion become a style statement
May we think of others' betterment
And adopt it as our definition

Lend your time, give a patient hearing
The world is grieving
Show empathy, be caring

What you sow, you shall reap
Sow love, love you shall receive
It will be your treasure forever to keep

Spread good cheer
To all near and dear
In this mission persevere

The world is in need of Compassion
Let us make it a passion
Let us make it a trending fashion!

55. FERRYING FUTURE

Be the Guiding Light
To your children
Open up their minds and hearts
To discovery through exploration

Be a Mentor
Let Mother Nature be their Nurturer
While the Wind shows them direction
To a life of fulfilment

Let them feel the strength
Of the shoulders they will stand upon
As Destiny unfolds its grand plans
'Cause each child holds our future in his hands!

56. PAPER BOAT DREAMS

A rare visit to the attic
A childhood storybook I picked
Began flipping through tales of fairies and ogres

A folded paper boat that had been anchored within
Found sudden release and fell on my feet
Prompting a treasure of remembrances…..

Curly hair, dark eyes sparkling bright
Carefully folding paper in many folds
Smoothening the edges with soft hands

A dreamer creating a dream
Of travels through flowing waters
Shadows falling in the azure aqua surface

It would discover new lands where happiness would be the norm
The sky would be filled with rainbows
Green meadows would be joyful playgrounds

A charming smile would play upon each lip
Butterflies would flit from flower to flower
Sweet bird sounds would rule the air

Maybe a call had interrupted my visions of Utopia
Maybe reality dawned…
A paper boat does not sail for long

Memories triggered brought me cheer galore
I had been born a romantic
Can anyone ask for more?!

57. THERE'S WONDER IN EVERYTHING I SEE

When I see life having emerged from life
In the form of an angel in the mother's fold
I am awestruck by the powers that be

Perfect features: twinkling eyes
Upturned nose, sunlit smile
Legs kicking energetically

In tandem there is life springing in nature
Pearly raindrops feed the saplings
As the red vented bulbul shields the young ones

Thread like rivulets find their way downhill
To meet the flowing river on the way to the sea
Life will follow it in its path

Beautiful life forms will surface
The cycle of life will continue to evolve
There's wonder in everything I see!

58. DEATH

Death, thou eternal Stalker!
You Watch every step
Of each being
Till destiny is fulfilled.
Then you fall in step,
Become a companion
To lead the soul
Towards the path
Of light Divine
And eternal Peace!

59. FEEDING THE DEVIL

She lay in the scarlet warmth, cosy, snug, contented, feeling cared
for
She heard her mother whisper sweetly to her
A nose, a mouth, ears, intestines, brain appeared slowly
Then grew tiny hands and feet that kicked and stretched
Small hiccups escaped her as she smiled - at peace within the
vermillion surroundings
In happiness she threw her legs about, dreaming of all that
awaited her

Angry voices heard now!!!

"Be peaceful!" she begged from within.

Suddenly she gasped as she felt a tug at her throat
In panic, she wanted to cry out loud
But.....
She was abruptly yanked, cruelly slashed away from her lifeline
Pulled out aggressively and thrown mercilessly into sudden
darkness

Where she lay gasping, her newly formed innocent eyes filled
with terror
Till they closed forever

A life with infinite potential waiting to conquer this earth
Remorselessly cut short
By hands that held power!
Was it punishment for being a girl?
Or was it the DEVIL feeding off our prejudice?

60. TRUE EUPHORIA

Thin parallel white lines
A deep inhalation
Suspension of disbelief
Distorted sense of reality
Fast track to Euphoria!

Stimulation
Levitation
Alleviation
Elevation
Kaleidoscopic vision!

Increased dependence
Loss of Concentration
Addiction
Depression
Violence!

A reassuring arm across the shoulder
A warm hug in times of fear
A kind ear to the near and dear
An effort to endear

Euphoria of love forever!

61. EXPECTATION

Burning Passion
Unfulfilled Ambition
Unrealised Mission
Instant Gratification
Assumption and anticipation
Without realization

Existence is not a straight walk
Or an easy call
Life throws curved balls
It is not a series
Of happy celebrations
On board bulletins

It is the courage
To smile
Through tears
Of facing fears
Of tackling adverse circumstances
Based on sound principles

Gathering wisdom along learning paths

To set realistic expectations!

62. EYES SAY IT ALL

(A humble tribute to our Saviours)

Beseeching eyes, anxious eyes
Appealing eyes, tearful eyes
Troubled eyes, desperate eyes
Melancholic eyes, mortified eyes

Eyes full of happiness
Cheerful eyes, hopeful eyes
Beaming eyes, ecstatic eyes
Sparkling eyes, jubilant eyes

Eyes unspeaking, silent
Yet expressive
Reflecting every emotion
Speaking louder than words can express

All eyes look deeply into your eyes
Searching for answers only you know
Relieved at discovering hope
Traumatised when there seems none

In whose eyes do you search
For love, for understanding
For warmth, for strength
For sustenance, for endurance?

Let our eyes be those that look up to
And venerate you, our dear Care Givers
To fill your lives with love and deference
So you may heal all you touch!

63. FORGING WOMEN POWER

The bride looked ravishingly radiant in red
Her eyes sparkled brighter than the ruby studded necklace
clutching her neck.
The proud mother sat opposite, stealing the last few precious
minutes before she departed
She hugged her daughter and made an affectionate hand gesture
to ward away the evil eye

The bride held on to her mother and whispered,
"Share some pearls of wisdom with me dear mother, so that I
may make a happy home."

Overcome with emotion and with tears in her eyes, the mother
replied,
"A woman not only lays the foundation of happiness of her
family; she is the backbone of the society."
"Your children will be the future generation. Educate them and
give them good values."
"The daughters you bear will forge the link of women power."

*"The sons will reap the benefit of learning from learned women
and become valuable citizens."*

*The young girl on the threshold of a new life absorbed the
teachings of her mother, her Guru.
She understood well the mantle of responsibility the universe had
placed on her.*

*The bride stood straight, looked deep into her mother's eyes and
folded her hands in reverence.
"I am the daughter of a woman of substance!" she said.
"I promise to carry forward the legacy bestowed upon me to
ensure wellbeing on the earth."*

*With that, the 'newly wed to be' fell upon the feet of her senior
and continued,
"Bless me my mother, my teacher, my saviour!"
"Place your gentle hand upon my head to give me strength to stay
strong.'
"Bestow upon me your divine grace so that I may bring pride
upon womanhood."*

64. GARDEN OF EDUCATION

(A tribute to all teachers)

Tiny seedlings
Require tender care and warm feelings
In the carefully planned nursery are tended
Before being cautiously transplanted

Nurturing becomes the key to all growth
Teachers are the gardeners that live by the oath
Of unprejudiced and impartial fostering
For those placed in their safe keeping

Teachers are motivators
They are cultivators
Of discipline and training
Who supervise growth of learning

Mentors they are
They hold and scaffold
Recognising each individual potential

They impart lessons that are experiential

Gurus of true knowledge
They invigorate and encourage
Their gardens are green spaces of inspiration
They are sculptors, their wards are their creation

Maestros at composing
Their compositions are awesome
For they bloom and blossom
In the bountiful garden of erudition!

65. CLOUDS OF IMAGINATION

My darling Angel
Let your head remain in the Misty wisps
For therein lies the Land of Creativity
Play with the ever forming and transforming
Clouds of imagination
And weave them into wondrous shapes
That your dreams are made of!

Keep your feet firmly on the ground
For they will lead you
To the path you destine for yourself!
Dream on my precious.....
Let not the world weigh down
Your fantastic fantasies

For it is those like thy enlightened self
Who rise above the others
To carry our Present
Into a glorious, haloed Future!

66. THE HIGHWAY DIARIES

4 AM - It's been a long night
Heavy trucks thundering up and down
I think I need to stretch my back
In a lighter vein- I am quite a stretch you know!

6 AM – The stubble burning smoke has formed a thick screen
There's a drunk maniac tearing up my North side
And a speed junky coming from the Southern end
Aaaah! As I feared.......

6. 30 AM -A pile-up now! Twenty-eight vehicles in all!!
I am strewn with shards of glass and spatters of blood
There's a child screaming for his mother, while a motor cycle is
burning
Do you think these people are carrying valid licenses?

12 Noon – The sun is shining hard on my face
Myriad patterns of hot air melt my surface
I need more trees I shout…

An empty bag of chips is hurled out of a window to muffle my
voice!

5 PM - I spot my favourite kind of travellers
A family singing merrily. What bliss!
It gives me hope that the night to follow
Will not be filled with horrors of senseless deaths!

67. IGNITE A SPARK

Inflame those embers of desire
Before they turn to ash
Lie they glowing and glimmering
Smouldering and simmering
Red illuminated dots
Escaping their bounds
Like fireflies afloat on a summer night

Let the winds of determination and resolve
Stoke the red-hot appetency
With your quest for conquest

Ignite a spark
Give birth to a flame of gold
Rejuvenate, aspire for more
Become a beacon
Enkindle your soul
Drive away darkness like it never existed

Transform into a light house
Radiant and luminous
Be a guiding light, construct a path of aureate sprinkles

That glows even in the darkness of the night!

68. IMAGES AND INVOCATION

Warm breath forms a circular pattern on the window
His nose is pressed against it as his eyes sparkle and dance in
excitement
A train journey!
Bliss unparalleled!!

Electric wires whiz past moving in perfect rhythm to the clickety
clackety of the wheels
Magical visions appear and disappear like images being viewed
through a bioscope
Fields of green stand tall crowned in harvest gold
Many a stream and rivulet shine in sparkling silver like a
treasure box thrown open
Ponds throng with sprightly scantily clad lads making a splash in
the cool waters as the buffaloes struggle to keep their space

A grinding halt with sparks flying, a result of friction of wheels
and the track
At the station now and the air is abuzz with sounds of various
decibels and a multitude of smells

A wave of people rush to clamber causing an amusing tussle with
those disembarking
Clink of cold drink bottles, steam from hot tea, sweetmeats in
competition with salty savouries....
A child at the breast, a young man giving support to his aging
father: a life beginning, a life concluding!

Time consumes distance
The blue sky starts to blush pink
Stars begin peeping as the moon keeps vigil from above
The rocking motion lulls all to the world of dreams
Lights of yellow are subdued, all is quiet other than the steady
drum beat of motion
But sleep eludes the lovable five seasons old traveller as he
watches lit up homes filing past like a row of fireflies

The odyssey will keep him captivated all night through
His mother quietly watches his fascination with the world
outside the window
A silent prayer rises from within her
May the Almighty be his shepherd as he journeys through
life........

69. THE PURSUIT OF LOVE

A quest for the pinnacle of romance
Like looking for a pot of gold
At the end of a rainbow
Riding an arched spectrum of vivid hues
Each shade shaping stimulation
Heightening expectation
Enhancing anticipation
Evoking passion

The desire for destination
An agony and an ecstasy
A journey for an oasis
To fulfil an unquenching thirst
The mind racing towards the goal
The heart embracing the voyage
The head conjuring images
Of immeasurable joy

Will the longing culminate in eternal bliss
Or does euphoric love

Exist in enhanced sensations
Of intoxicating adventure in the pursuit?!

70. IT'S ALL ABOUT PRIDE

Noticing the lines of concern on the forehead
The mother ran her loving hands through
The shiny ringlets of her pride and joy
Smiled she and asked the cause

Said he,
"I am confused Ma."
I read today that
Pride comes before a fall."

"Should I give up
All pride in my being,
And be proud that I am
No longer proud?"

Replied she,
"Not if you are its master
And take pride
As motivation

To do good for others"

"Careful not to let
It be lead you
To the path
Of false superiority"

"For false pride
Will lead you to
To a path of
Insecurity and loneliness"

"Dominate your emotions
Let self-respect be your pride
Dignify your life with self-worth
To give your utmost
To the good of humanity!"

71. JUNG-e-VAIRAV, the saga of the brave Parsi women

The Battle of Variav was fought by the brave Parsi women on the banks of the river Tapti, in the small village of Variav, near Surat. The story of their heroism is sung in Gujarati folk songs till this day.

The Raja of Ratanpur, was enraged with the Parsis of Variav because they refused to pay the revenue 'mehesul'. In order to enforce his unjust demand, he would send mercenaries or 'garasias' to claim the mehesul but their attacks were always repulsed by the Parsi men of Variav.

Disaster struck the day the men had gone away to a distant village to celebrate the feast of 'gambhar' leaving behind the women and the elderly.......

The wily spy approached the King and whispered
'Never will there be as opportune a moment'
A slow smile of revenge spread on the royal face
He raised his hand in signal to his blood thirsty troops

Rays of the sun danced on the ripe crop in the field

The air rang with laughter but short-lived was happiness
As the horizon darkened with swirls of dark dust
Warning the arrival of danger and death!

Unfazed, Navaz, the brave woman shouted:
"We will bear arms and protect our own!
Tie your hair, wear a helmet, cover your face!
Mount the horses! Attack!!"

Blood curdling war cries rose
Headless bodies of men fell
The earth was soaked in red
The enemy turned their back to retreat

Alas! A blow dislodged a helmet
Tumbling down came a cascade of hair
"Cowards! Do not go down to housewives!"
Cried the men as they re-grouped for a fresh attack

Fate had played its cruel card
It had snatched defeat from the jaws of victory!
Surrender to dishonour they never would
Alongside were the flowing waters of the Tapti

Letting out a furious cry of the victorious
The brave Parsi women plunged into the rushing waters

Whose anger and helplessness rose in frothing eddies
As it gathered them in its loving embrace forever!

72. IMMORTAL LOVE

Our love is eternal
It is unbounded, abundant and infinite
It is immeasurable and timeless
It has withstood the test of time

In the beginning, it was just You and me
You infused life into me creating me in a unique mould
You set me free to fulfil the chosen destiny
To live a life unhindered thereafter

In the breezy whisper of a zephyr, I hear you
In the morning rays of the sun, I read your message
Every drop of rain falling from the heavens above
Is a reminder of promises I made to you

Blinded by desire, blindsided by ego
I falter, I lose sight of my goal
I introspect, I correct course
And yet again I lose track

My Lord, my saviour be always by my side
Shield me under the umbrella of your protection

Hold me in the palm of your hands forever more
Our bond is perennial and imperishable – just You and me!

73. LANGUAGE, LITERATURE AND SOCIETY: QUEST FOR UTOPIA!

Expressions needed expression!
Joy, sorrow, love, anguish
Eyes said it all.
The hands wanted to give a hand.
Expressions found pictorial images
On Cave walls, surfaces and trees.
Sound wanted to join in..
Expressions began resonating!

Experiences needed expression
Stories needed telling….
Gestures, sounds began creating
Vivid tales of wonder.
Earth revolved;
Time evolved
Intelligence developed

Finer sensitives began emerging….

Sounds found alphabets
Alphabets strung together in a rhythm
Made words.
Mutual understanding,
Common acceptance of communication
And a miracle….
Lo and behold,
Language was born!

Minds were swayed,
Intellect found escape,
Thoughts of society were mirrored,
Literature found itself in reflection.
Independence of thought
Brought revolutions.
Geographical boundaries were redefined.

Shits of power took place
Like a see saw out of control.
Some gains, some losses,
Tears and laughter!
The struggle continues…
Literature mirrors truth,
Truth is mirrored by literature

Societies remain dynamic!

Quest for Utopia
Through expression and the expressed continues....

74. LOHRI: THE JOYFUL BLAZE OF HARVEST

The sun begins it's Uttarayana
Its golden rays cast a magic spell
Over the vast expanses of wheat fields
And each grain captures the radiance
Emitting it back manifold
Creating a brilliant, shimmering carpet of gold

The spontaneous gladness of the farmer at such splendour
Finds it's manifestation
In imitating fires which throw up their arms
Spreading star like embers of red into the skies
The fires of warmth and light
The fires of Lohri!

The atmosphere resounds with lyrical renditions of
Sunder munderiye ho!
Tera kaun vichara ho!
Dullah Bhatti walla ho!
A song sung in sweet Punjabi

In praise of Dulla Bhatti
Who robbed from the rich and helped the poor

The wafting music stirs memories of childhood
Of running unhindered in the street
With the wind caressing every curl in my hair
Of songs sung with young companions
Of sheer joy and laughter at receiving a few coins
In appreciation from the listeners

The dholis beat feverishly
And the young, old, men, women, children
Newly wedded, lately born
Dance around the fires to the frenzied rhythm
Offering gifts of til, nuts and popcorn into the flames
That seem to cavort, frolic and prance

The children add to the charm
Their faces are aglow with excitement
They have learnt without being told
About the safety measures that must be adhered to
That pleasure and responsibility are inseparable
And the delights of celebrating festivities as a community

I stand captivated
Caught in the everlasting moment
Of the enchanting evening

With the sacred prayer upon my lips:
"Aadar aye dilather jaye"
May honour come and poverty vanish!

• 144 •

75. LIFE IS A MIRAGE

Our sense of ownership
Of this material world
Is as true as a mirage
As you approach it
And get closer
The images of grandeur vapourise
Truth stares at you
Humbling you into
The realization that
Life itself is an illusion
All our possessions are material
And temporary
We are transients
Here today
And gone tomorrow

Make your life sublime
Live not in the impermanent
Reality lies in the Eternal!

76. LIFE OUR GREATEST TEACHER

The lesson of life
Unfolds page by page
Each day a story hidden from us
Of sorrow, happiness, love, sacrifice
Travails, tribulations, turbulence
Or trials we would withstand that day

Life is a voyage spanning a lifetime
There are no road signs or warnings
The beginning is unclear
The journey tough, end unknown
One road leads to another
And one must chart out one's own path

A path that may lead us to crossroads
Of indecision, fear, insecurity
Yet travel we must, to stop is not an option
Victorious sometimes, often defeated
We fall, we rise, we try again
And life continues to be our teacher!

77. WE SHALL OVERCOME

The golden sun of wellness shall rise
The Pink Dawn of well-being shall spread its wondrous streak
across the horizon
We shall overcome!

Like an untrained wire walker
I am resolute to sustain the balance of my life
To not fall off the rope
When You shake it violently
To test my strength

My steps may falter
My faith remains strong
Strong winds augment my ordeal
I hold my head high
I trust my feet to hold their grip

Songs of Victory shall fill the air
Agony will be forced to retreat in defeat
Generations to come will be inspired

The fight is on
Let us stay strong

The golden sun of wellness shall rise
The Pink Dawn of well-being shall spread its wondrous streak
across the horizon
We shall overcome!

78. VISIONS OF LAVENDER

(A tribute to a street artist)

She stood at her usual spot in the Artists' Bay
Next to her the gurgling fountain splashed encouragement
Her artwork on display depicted the beautiful Lavender in
various manifestations
The flowers, her inspiration, the depictions of her past
Were imprinted indelibly in her awareness

Images flashed across her vivid mind as she faced the canvas
Her consciousness was flooded with memories
The mind froze with one frame
In tandem with the recollection, flew the brush across the board
She smiled as her paint brought the stretched tarp to life

Shades of violet were splashed like scattered, glittering amethysts
Thick florets of Lavender surrounding the green stems appeared
magically
Shaded in different hues by dappled sunshine filtering through
the scattered cumulus

*Wondrously appeared a charming young girl running across the
field of lilac flowers
Her blond hair flying in the wind claiming unhindered joy*

*Unnoticed stood passers-by, now rooted - transfixed by her
passion
Admirers mesmerised by her evocative depiction
They applauded as she sighed happily and rested her life-giving
brush
She turned and took a bow, her sparkling unseeing eyes filled
with tears of gratitude
Beholden to reminiscences that found vision in strokes of Colour
Purple*

79. BROOMING BEATS

Battery charged; ear plugs on
Where's the broom
And the mop?
Let me put the music on

'Teen taal' is my beat of choice
Ready to clean and to swap
Let me sing and lend my voice
As I cleanse every spot

Sixteen beats
Will be the rhythm loop
Of the song
And my sponge

'Dhaa dhin dhin dhaa'
Sweep, brush, clean and wash
'Dhaa, dhin dhin dhaa'
Scour, scrape, scrub and rake
'Dhaa tin tin taa'
Wipe, dust, whisk and rub
'Taa dhin dhin dhaa'

Polish, rub and I buff

The rhythmic melody is done
Dust in my home is none
Blemish free is my abode
At peace is my soul!

80. GROWING FROM STRENGTH TO STRENGTH

(A tribute to motherhood)

My world rests on the legacy
You bestowed upon me
Your loving hands held mine
With warmth and support
In my lowest moments
Your healing touch
Rejuvenated joy and faith in life

Yours is the legacy
I build upon
I seek your blessings constant
And draw strength from you
So that I take forward
Your learnings
To those who will come after

Each wrinkle of your hand

Tells a story of your sacrifice
Your selflessness and devotion
To my wellbeing
I place my hand upon yours
As a pledge and to forge a link
To grow from strength to strength

81. LOVE AT FIRST SIGHT

I am True Love
Ask not for my definition
For then I will be bound
Imprison not, nor confine me
For I will be immured
In solitary confinement

I am Divine Intervention
I am Eternal
When I conquer at first sight
Lovers surrender to me without a fight
I flow uninterrupted through them
And empower their senses

My strength is limitless
My reach boundless
Let my embrace warmly clasp
Every being, spirit, soul
Declare me the Ruler

Relinquish your heart to me

Then there will always be sunshine
Rainbows will cover the sky
Hatred will slink away
Never to be found again!

82. ETERNAL LOVE

It was a long and cold winter night, the sky was dark outside
Her asthma was acting up, she had been coughing for the last
few minutes
The pitcher by the bedside had become cold by now.
'A glass of warm water would calm her down,' he thought
The quilt felt warm and comforting, the mind struggled
Ever so slowly he got up and trudged to the kitchen, wincing as
sharp pain rose up his legs
Moments later he stood by her bedside, "Here my dear, sip some
warm water."

Opening her eyes slowly, she struggled up to gratefully accept the
soothing liquid
He sat down on the edge of her bed to rub her back in between
the hot sips
Presently she put her hand on his and said, "I am feeling much
better
Your knee must be hurting in this cold. Let me rub some balm
on you."
The skyline was beginning to lighten up when they snuggled back
into the quilt

To get some sleep before they woke up to add another day of togetherness
To fifty years, three months and twenty days!

83. LUMINESCENT FUTURE

As he poured champagne into the fluted glass
On the eve of twenty five years of togetherness
The bubbles erupted into a coruscant life
Prompting shimmering memories
Of our Silver Past on to Golden Times....

I had been laughing superficially at a poor joke
When I spotted him
Eyes had met across a room
No sparks had flown, no music was heard
But the moment froze in the mind

Time flew by
Met again at a 'Save the Earth' Campaign
Green conversations followed
Mutual respect and admiration grew
Our relationship grew as did the cause

Pink was the sky
The Laburnum chandelier blooms

Shed an aureate petal as a divine blessing
As we decided to share the future
Binding our lives and hearts forever and ever!

84. I CAN FEEL YOU

A momentary sensation
Like the presence of a gentle breeze
Like the flutter of a pretty butterfly
My heart fills up with joy unbound

I can feel you

You and I bound together
Beholden by a bond sacred
You and I are soulmates
Of the bountiful energies of this universe

I can feel you

I whisper to you
In a language of love
That is only ours
To speak and understand

I can feel you

You and I breathe as one

Your breath and mine intertwined
My beautiful child
I can feel you within me
Till I hold you in my arms!

85. GLORIOUS AUTUMN

She sat under the Chinar
A smile of gratitude playing upon her lips
Autumn had set in
The colour of the Chinar leaves that had evolved to yellow
Shone burnt orange complimenting the shades of the setting sun
And would soon soundlessly fall, making way for the new greens

Her heart sang as the gentle zephyr carried
The sound of tinkling laughter
Of her grandchild playing at a distance
Her ribbon ensconced ringlets
Bouncing upon her tender shoulders
That would boldly bear the weight of the coming morrow

The gold rays of the departing sun
Dancing on the multi lobed leaves
Caught the luminescence of her silver strands
And shimmered like a heavenly crown
As nature paid homage

To the custodian of the emerging generation

Heavens radiated blessings that divine evening
For both victors who had successfully played their second innings
Fulfilled their destiny and kept their silent promise
Of staying firm and holding strong
To pass on the baton to their next of kin to lead the universe
Into a glorious future…..

86. MAHAN AATMA

The Palash had shaken off the summer inertia and begun to
paint the horizon with streaks of red
The fragrant and floral lawns of Birla House resounded with soft
chants
The devotees waited with quiet patience for an experience
sublime!
There was a ten minute delay, then He appeared.........

His frail form rested on the shoulders of his two disciples
Yet He was the strongest man the world had ever seen
His spectacled eyes mirrored a divine vision fulfilled
His toothless smile challenged the brilliance of the setting sun

A figure in Khaki parted the crowds and moved forward hands
folded
A cloud like a dark shadow passed overhead
One, Two, Three, Four
Hey Ram!!!!!!!

Ruby drops rained down awakening Creation from its state of
tranquillity
And the Mother opened her arms to hold her beloved son

In a close embrace softly whispering a call to return to her fold
Earth to Earth!

A son who had risen to become a father to a nation new born
Breathing his last had submitted himself for all eternity
Granting humanity the right to breathe
In complete Freedom!

87. MONOCHROME CITY

The City is grandiloquent and loquacious.
It speaks to me in elaborate and complex dialects

Its coruscating, brilliant, sparkling lights flash shimmering,
scintillating messages of splendour and grandeur
That transport the mind into luminescent spaces of wealth and
well-being
Fast cars, rock music, coiled bodies moving to rhythmic beats
Rich food, wine infested intimate conversations, loud carefree
laughter

In the shadows of glimmering bulbs exists a parallel universe
Of 'made up' faces, inviting gestures and 'come hither' smiles
In an area colour coded 'red' supporting the oldest 'bare all'
profession known to mankind
Aiming to sell false happiness for remittances to sustain survival

The morning brings the rays of golden sunshine
A race against time begins…..
Rush, rush, rush, beat the traffic, meet deadlines, strike deals

*The atmosphere is abuzz with 'money talks' in the new era of
'dog eat dog'*

*The shaded patches resound with hungry cries of children
smothered by impatient, blowing horns
Of hopeful migrants searching for an elusive life of comfort
Of rag pickers rushing to pick through the mountains of trash
Remnants of the hedonistic night reduced to humungous heaps*

*The colourful city a monochrome
It exists as an oxymoron in images of black and white and shades
of grey!*

88. MY SUNSHINE

You beat the morning light
To bring sunshine into my life
Tears of gratitude filled my eyes
A life had been born from a life
A life innocent
A life magnificent!

All of universe had shown me faith
I bowed my head in humbled state
Held my precious one in embrace
Whispered an ardent prayer
My Lord my invocations to hear
Give me strength for my fortune to bear

Came the answer to me in a soft whisper
Trust your instinct
Let truth guide your path
Be the guiding light to follow
Allow not doubt to shadow
It is a bond of selfless love

Let it flow uninterrupted in forms unseen

For it to be born again and again

89. CHOOSE TO BE A SERAPHIM

She lay in the scarlet warmth, cosy, snug, contented and cared for
She had heard her mother whisper sweetly to her and when she
was restless soft music had filtered into her cocoon
In happiness she threw her legs about, dreaming of all that
awaited her
Suddenly she gasped as she felt a tug at her throat, she panicked
and wanted to cry out loud

Outside in the real world, her struggle was noticed by her
saviour , the young intern
Within no time the chord that was threatening her was cut by a
life giving surgeon's knife!
Wailing in triumph she entered this realm looking into the
tear-filled, grateful eyes of her mother
A life with infinite potential was born, claiming this earth-her
ground to conquer!

In the vicinity gurgled another life that had been growing
steadily within every day
A nose, a mouth, ears, intestines, brain appearing slowly

Then tiny hands and feet that kicked and stretched
Small hiccups escaping her as she smiled, tranquil, at peace in
the vermillion surroundings

She was abruptly yanked, cruelly slashed away from her lifeline
Pulled out aggressively and thrown mercilessly into sudden
darkness
Where she lay gasping, her newly formed innocent eyes filled
with terror......... till they closed forever
A life with infinite potential waiting to conquer this earth was
remorselessly cut short by a killer surgeon's knife!

A life saved: A life destroyed
By hands that held the tools and the power
To give all: Yet it took all!!
Was it punishment for being a girl? Was it prejudice? Was it a
mindless act of greed?

Bound You are, our guardian, by the Hippocratic oath to live
true and give life
Denigrate, dishonour not your God like power
Buy not detestation, condemnation and shame
Allow us always to bow down in obeisance for you are worthy of
worship!

90. OLIVE GREEN: THE COLOUR OF UNITY IN DIVERSITY

Bravery is his definition
Resilience is his greatest strength
Patience is his power
Love for his country is his strongest emotion

The nation looks at him for protection
And he answers each call unfailingly
Without a thought for his dear ones
He sacrifices himself for ours

He is our guardian angel
We owe him each moment of peace
His blood is purest
Because it flows to cleanse evil

He wears Olive Green with pride
Whether Hindu, Sikh or Christian
From the North, South, West or East

For OG is the colour of Unity, in diversity

He fights till his last breath making his life sublime
Comes home he swathed in tri-colour
A reminder to a nation in debt
That dedicating his life as a True Indian is a Soldier's Foremost
Honour!

91. OPEN YOUR ARMS TO JOY

Embrace life with all your being
Absorb and relish each happy moment
Shed a tear and wipe away shadows of sadness
Let your emotions flow unhindered

Like a brimming river
Let the flow of unstoppable time
Carry away all that was
To make room for the present and the coming morrow

Let not life get confined
To reliving happenings of the gone by
And effectively obstruct
New dawns and fresh beginnings

Like a bunch of colourful balloons
Floating upwards towards the azure
Breathe positivity into the beyond
Let the Universe smile eternal divinity upon you!

92. NO ONE KNOWS MY PAIN – I DO!

There exists an umbilical bond between the heart and the mind
The mind that is the awareness zone of all experiences
Keeps a note of all happenings much like a personal diary
To which only the heart has access

Agony is the strongest emotion the heart bears
Misery torments and breaks through all barriers
Encompassing and afflicting torture in totality
Submerging one's entire self into excruciating anguish

The resulting pain is ours to own
It consumes and activates all senses
It is like the roaring, swirling dark thunder
Resulting in deafening and blinding lightening

A barrage of intense sentiments
Pour out like heavy rain bearing clouds
Laying bare, exposing the buried festering wounds
That are torn open and begin to bleed

Battered, bruised, sobbing, heaving
The body lies vented at last
Finally allowing healing sunshine
To rejuvenate, recreate, regenerate and repair!

93. PARADISE

A place beyond the pearly gates?
Or a state of being euphoric?

The unknown
Or the now and wow!

Will it be reached by.....
The pilgrim climbing icy heights in search of the Almighty
Or the ever thirsty drunk headed for the bar?

Will glory be found....
In the sounds of temple bells?
Or in the tinkling laughter of a young one?

Does it exist in...
In the heaving waters of the ocean
Or sighting of an oasis by a desert traveller?

Is it felt by....
Acquiring an expensive asset
Or in the kiss of a lover?

Is it experienced by….
Settling in a prosperous land?
Or by coming back into the folds of the motherland?

Is it blissful….
To receive gifts aplenty?
Or to give selflessly?

The choice is ours
You look for your land of ecstasy
While I search for my own Heaven!

94. PATHS and DESTINATIONS

It was well begun
Now it is half done

Out of breath
From meeting expectations
Of others and Mine
I pause to think

I review, I rethink
I evaluate, I judge

Was it all worthwhile?
Did I do right?

The reply comes from within
Life has a guide map
Unknown to us
There are destinations we decide
But creation has its way

The past gave experiences to build upon
To recognise strengths and weaknesses

The present beckons
To take firm decisions
And build upon the strengths
To carve out a path culminating eternal bliss!

95. PEACE

Peace, thou flitting and elusive emotion
You seem to be a notion
Slipping away even before I realise your presence
Even though I hold you in great reverence

I seek, I search
You are always beyond reach
Just beyond my grasp
Though hard I try to clasp

Where lies the secret place where you hide?
I have explored far and wide
This game of hide and seek
Leaves me feeling lost and weak

A wisp of wind whispers in my ear
It seems you are not far but near
In my heart is your cove
Within me you await my love!

96. POWER OF THOUGHTS

The teacher was in meditation
The disciple sat patiently at his feet
He had come to look for answers
He had to channelise his wandering mind
Before his life lost all purpose and meaning.

The Guru opened his eyes at last.
With folded hands asked the disciple,
"O Divine Master I have come to you for guidance
I want to understand the power of thoughts."

Thus spoke the Learned One.
"All creations are powered by thoughts
Clear your head of all tangled webs
Destroy conflicting notions
Remove fear of failure
Canalise your creativity
Identify your vision
Manoeuvre your mind towards your perception

You shall see your guiding light."

The Great One paused a while and continued softly,
"Follow the illuminant beacon
Let discipline of action power the path of your vision
The energies of the Universe will come together
You will arrive at your goal!"

97. IT'S ALL ABOUT PRIDE

Noticing the lines of concern on the forehead
The mother ran her loving hands through
The shiny ringlets of her pride and joy
Smiled she and asked the cause

Said he,
"I am confused Ma."
I read today that
Pride comes before a fall."

"Should I give up
All pride in my being,
And be proud that I am
No longer proud?"

Replied she,
"Not if you are its master
And take pride
As motivation

To do good for others"

"Careful not to let
It be lead you
To the path
Of false superiority"

"For false pride
Will lead you to
To a path of
Insecurity and loneliness"

"Dominate your emotions
Let self-respect be your pride
Dignify your life with self-worth
To give your utmost
To the good of humanity."

98. THE NEXT CHAPTER

She steals a few minutes of quiet
To be by herself
And gather her thoughts
Thoughts that will find words
Words that will be inked in that diary
A diary that knows it all
She looks into the mirror
The image of a young bride
Looks back at her
Swathed in red
Glittering in gold from toe to head
Eyes shining with excitement of the undisclosed
A chapter of life is about to close
The known and familiar
Is about to change
To unknown and new beginnings
Once she crosses the threshold
Everything she was, will become her past
Her hand races across the pages noting her feelings
She is near the end

She flips to the next page to peek into her tomorrow
A blank white space stares back
She wishes she could read the invisible ink
That will reveal itself on the day yet to come

99. TRIUMPH OVER SAOMAI

*(This poem is a tribute to the 'never say die' spirit of the fearless
and valiant officer of the Indian Navy aboard a Destroyer
headed to China, caught mid sea by Typhoon Saomai 2000,
which was one of the most intense tropical storms of our times
causing several shipping accidents and fatalities.
In order to survive, the ship had to be kept moving with its head
facing the winds- an exercise requiring tremendous courage,
forbearance and technical skill as the engines and power
generators continuously failed, even as cracks developed and
water tried to overpower it)*

*The fiery ball of orange slowly took on a bronze hue
As it lingered on to watch the synchronised activity
Of men in immaculate crisp white working in a harmony
Born out of endless hours of painstaking training*

*The course was set, the powerful engines throbbed with power
As the majestic Destroyer of the Indian Navy eased off Mumbai
harbour*

*Its dark and brooding silhouette framed against the tangerine
tinted skies
And the waters of the Arabian Sea parted themselves in
obeisance*

*Onward it leapt on the undulating waves, unbeknownst
To it the winds had congregated elsewhere to test human
endurance
The calm rays of moonshine effectively hiding this secret
In the evenly breathing waters of the vast East China Sea*

*The dawn was swiftly kidnapped by unyielding, angry clouds
Brought on by bellowing winds hollering out a war cry
Working the mountainous waves into a frenzy to drown the ship
Like a bully forcefully dunking the head of a hapless swimmer
Surfaced the mighty vessel to take in life-saving breaths of air
Only to be thrown high and land back in a bone-jarring crash
The battle between Nature's unbridled fury and man had begun!
'Head to the Wind!' shouted the team of four hundred trapped
within*

*Saomai's cloud-filled eyes began to develop <u>concentric eyewalls</u>
The wrath of the tempest spun the ship to break its resistance
As the ocean became a hollow ready to swallow it
'Head to the Wind!' shouted the team of four hundred trapped
within*

Resolute, determined, unwavering in its purpose was the team
Of hundred and twenty led by the undaunted Senior engineer
Who battled on together for seven long unforgiving days and
nights
Keeping alive the wounded engines, defeating sea sickness and
disorientation

The surface split open many a times as the salty sea tried to gain
entry
Men fell and rose again uncomplainingly to the call of duty
The brave worked furiously to keep the groaning ship in
movement
For failure to move on ahead would mean total surrender

'Head to the Wind!' shouted joyously, the triumphant team of
four hundred
As the typhoon conceded defeat, retrieving its life-threatening
presence
Divinity smiled on twentieth September, the birthday of the
senior engineer
Offering a befitting salute to the brave heart saviour- my brother
Shailen!

100. IN CONVERSATION WITH THE WINTER BREEZE

The weary traveller felt the bitter bite of the winter breeze
As it swooshed past him and asked,
"O scathing cold breeze why do you hurt me so?"
Whistling a rasping tone, said the winter breeze,
"I represent the harsh truth
I am the reality tough to face
I mirror the struggles of life
I am the one who assesses your strength
I am the test of your endurance."

"Do you not repent the unpopular role of your existence?"
Asked the fatigued traveller.
"Oh, you read me wrong," replied the relentless Winter breeze
"I refine your soul
I make life's pleasures more pleasurable
I help discover inner strength
I create heroes from among the ordinary

I make conquest a celebration
Rue not my existence
Let your fortitude triumph
And emerge a glorious victor!"

101. SOMEDAY, SOMEWHERE

Someday, somewhere, someone
Cried out in pain
The wind carried the suffering
To unknown ears
The heart sent a message to the lips
The lips let out a prayer to heal

Someday, somewhere, someone
Heard a prayer of healing
The breeze lifted it to listening ears
The heart prompted the lips
The lips joined the prayer

Someday, somewhere, everyone
Will receive the prayer of healing
Softly fetched by the light zephyr
Many a prayer
Will simultaneously rise heavenwards
And the Earth shall heal!